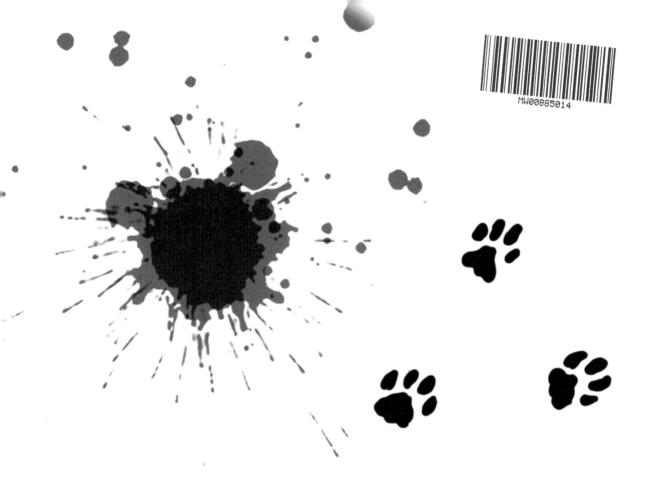

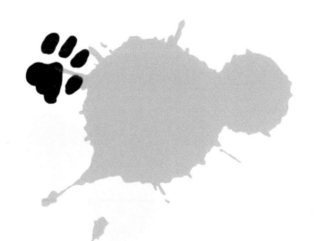

Once upon a time there was a little cat named Pixel.

He was cute and funny, but VERY naughty.

He lived in a house with two people and two dogs,

and he had all sorts of adventures.

Meet Pixel.

When he was very small,

he loved books, even though he couldn't read.

Instead, he liked to nap on them

so no one else could read them either.

As he got bigger, Pixel got braver.

One day, he tried to get a closer look at the fish.

That was a <u>very</u> soggy adventure!

Pixel wasn't discouraged though. Not at all!

Soon he was stealing food from the great big dogs.

Poor hungry hound dogs!

No, Bad Cat, Don't do that.

Pixel liked to be the center of attention,

so he got in the way a lot.

It's hard to see through even a very small cat.

Curious Pixel liked to push things off the countertop,

just to see what would happen.

Oh what a mess!

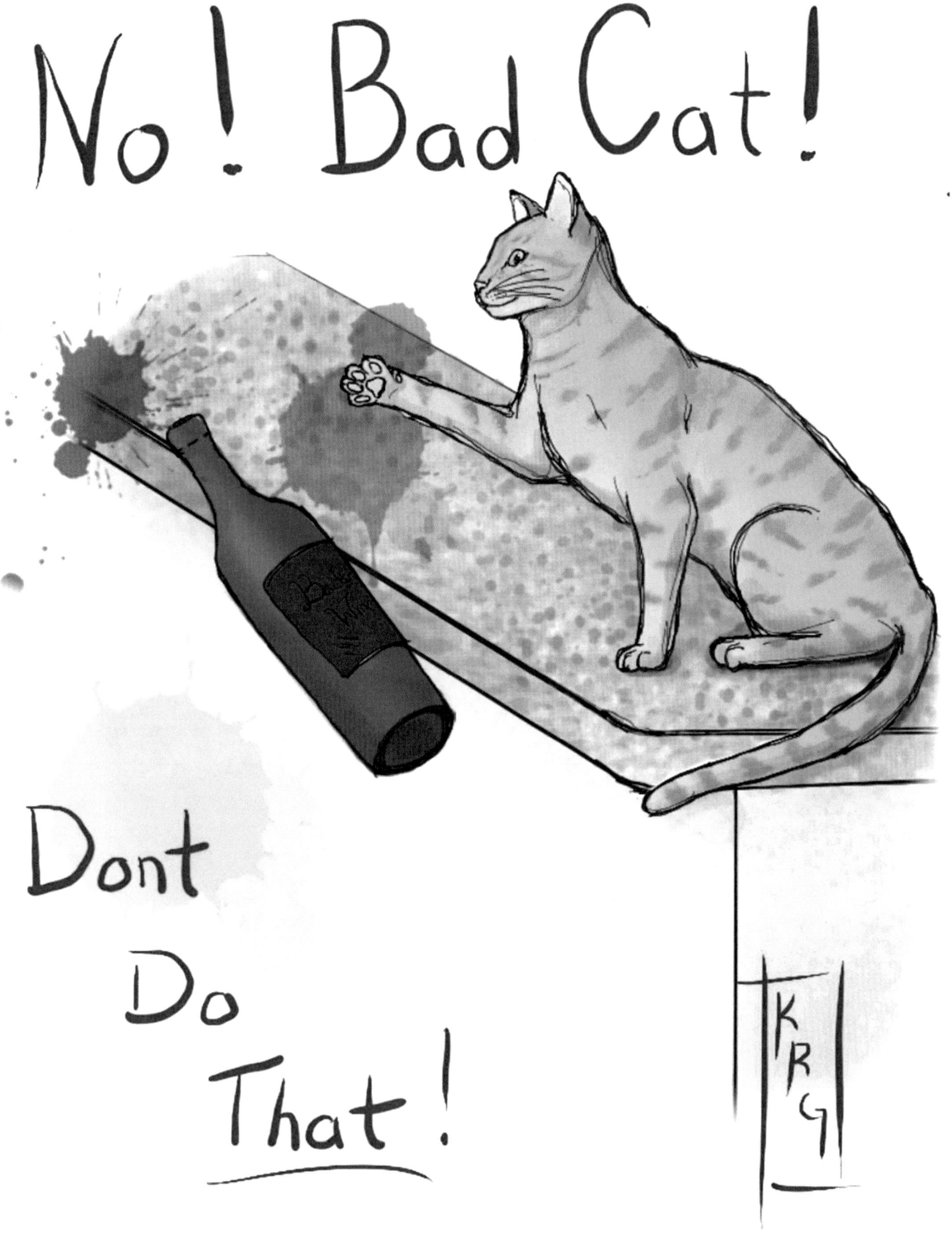
No! Bad Cat!
Dont Do That!
KRG

One day Pixel thought

he'd try a new use for potted plants.

It was **NOT** a good idea.

Next, he thought he'd try to eat one.

But houseplants are to look at, not to eat.

So that didn't work out very well.

Since he couldn't eat the plant,

Pixel decided to try eating at the dinner table.

But that wasn't allowed either...

...so he thought he'd pack himself a lunch.

Too bad the lunch already belonged to someone else.

No sandwiches for bad cats!

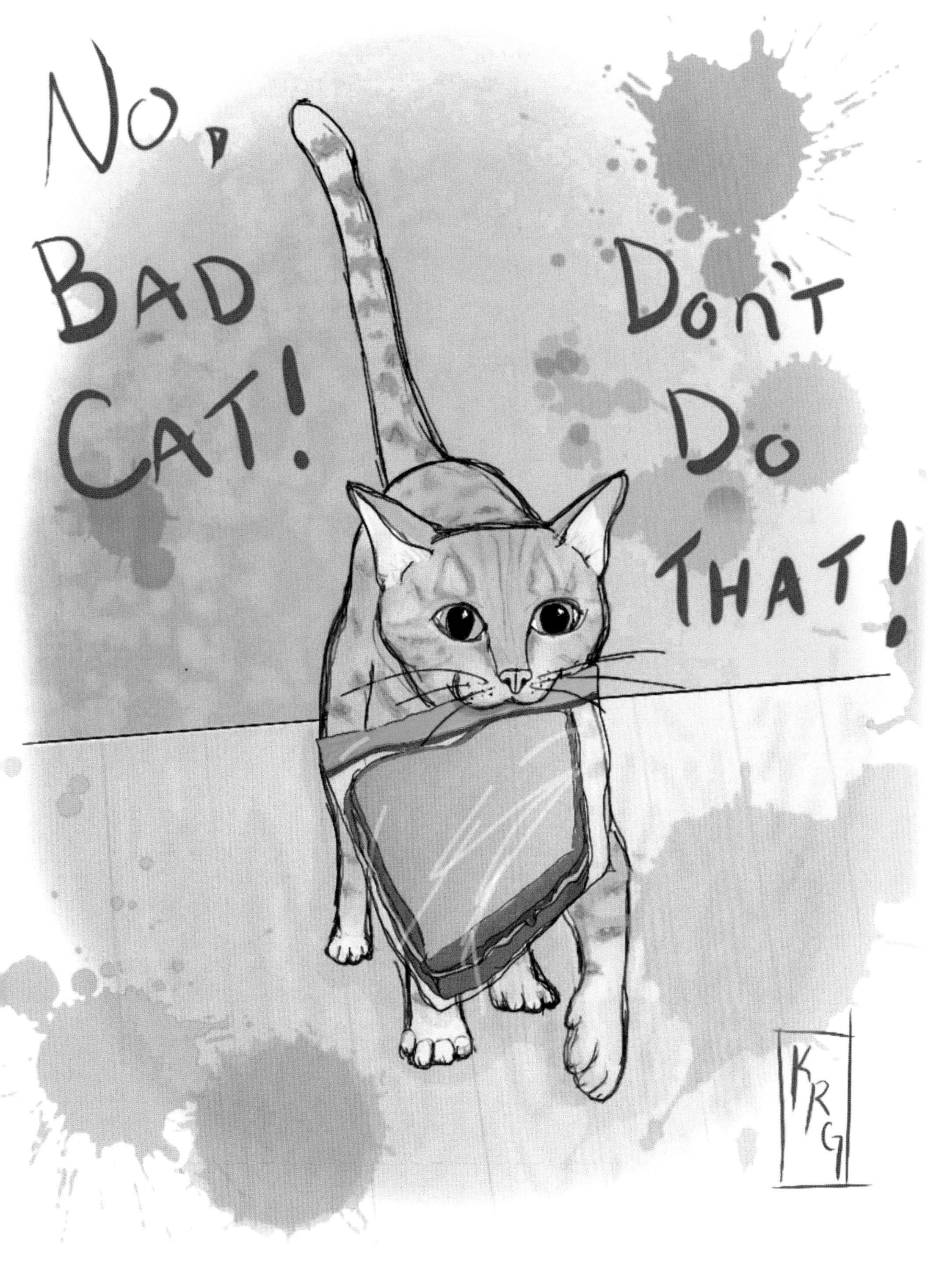
No, BAD CAT!
Don't Do THAT!
KRG

Pixel had some other adventures too.

He found out that it's not good to jump onto the toilet.

Especially when others are around.

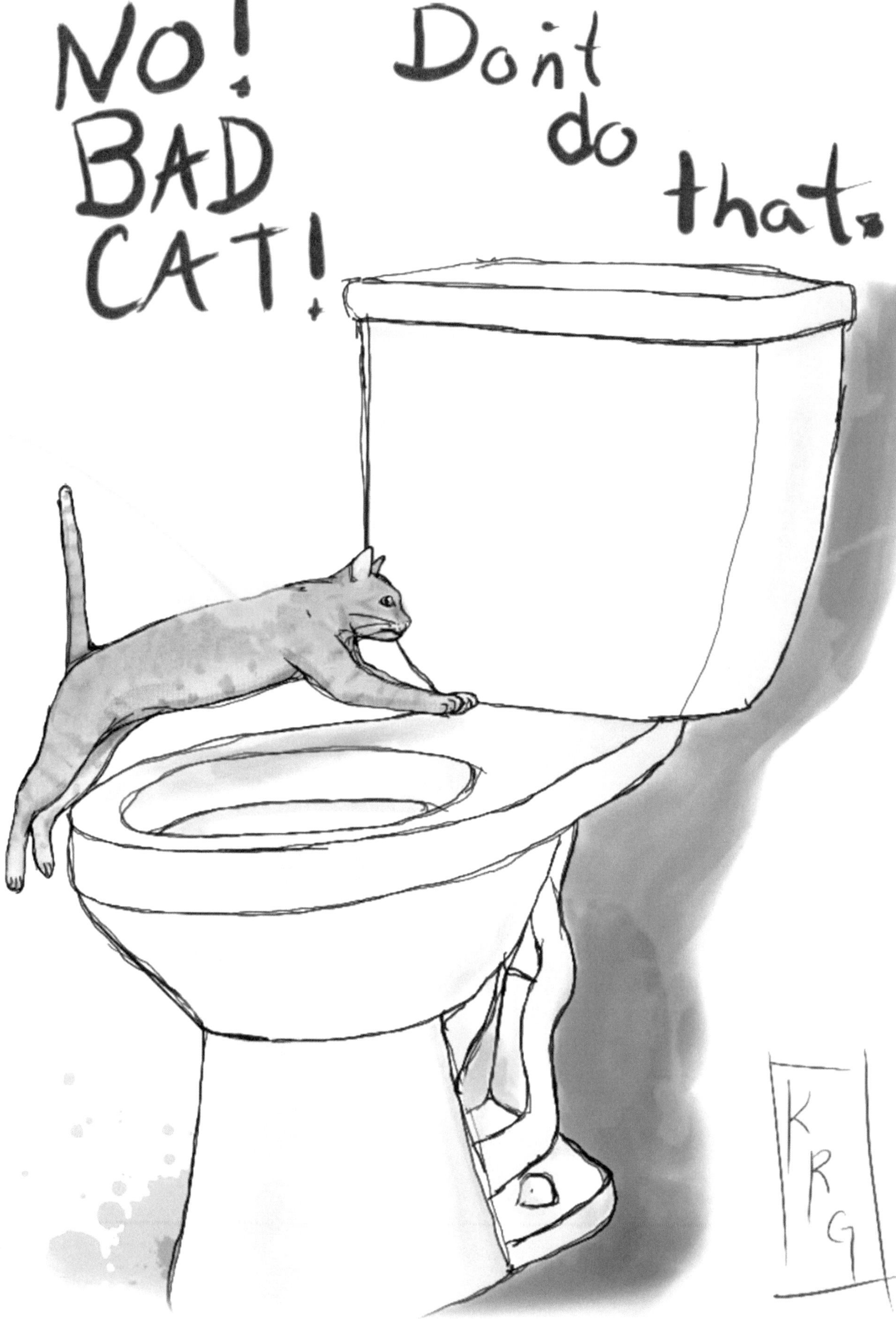
NO! BAD CAT!
Don't do that.
KRG

He discovered that yoga mats are soft and squishy,

but people like them better when they're in one piece

So he looked for other things to scratch.

But sometimes copying people
can get a cat in trouble.

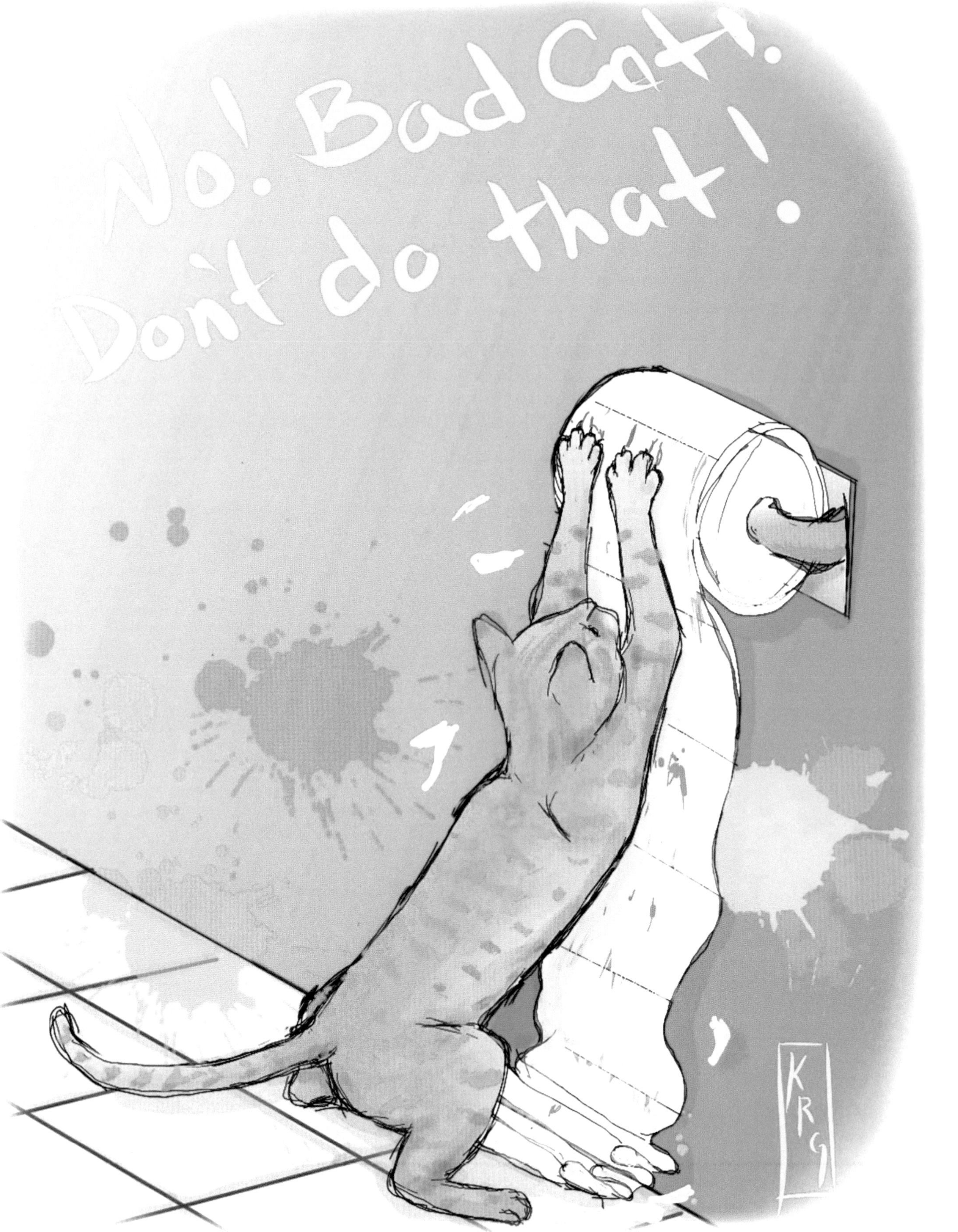
No! Bad Cat!
Don't do that!
KRG

And sometimes even things that look like cat toys...

Are not.

How's a cat supposed to know?

As he got older, Pixel tried to develop hobbies.

But for some reason they never worked out.

He thought about leaving home...

...but that wasn't a good plan either.

So he went back to indoor entertainment.

Sometimes that could be a little scary.

But Pixel still wanted to be involved.

And when all the day's adventures were done,

Pixel was one tired little cat!

But he still liked to spend time with his friends.

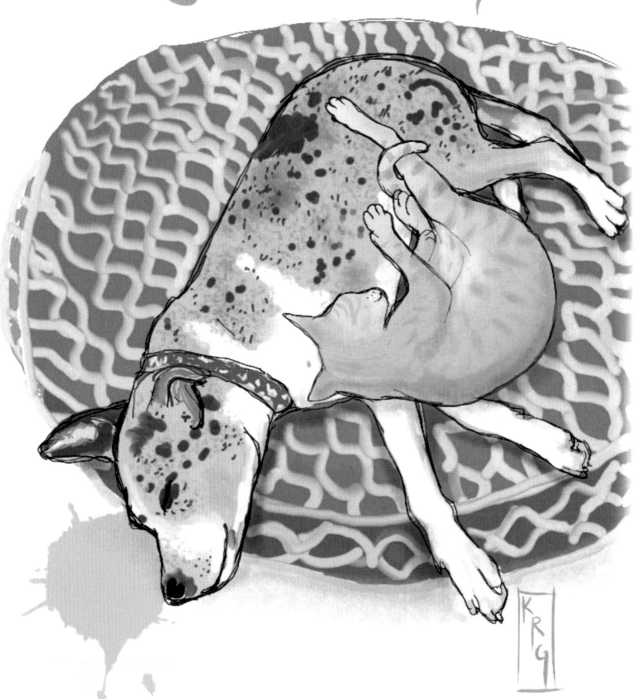

Made in the USA
Lexington, KY
17 September 2017